HOW TO SURVIVE A
BLIZZARD

KENNY ABDO

Bolt!

An Imprint of Abdo Zoom
abdopublishing.com

abdopublishing.com

Published by Abdo Zoom, a division of ABDO, P.O. Box 398166, Minneapolis, Minnesota 55439. Copyright © 2019 by Abdo Consulting Group, Inc. International copyrights reserved in all countries. No part of this book may be reproduced in any form without written permission from the publisher. Bolt!™ is a trademark and logo of Abdo Zoom.

Printed in the United States of America, North Mankato, Minnesota.
052018
092018

THIS BOOK CONTAINS RECYCLED MATERIALS

Photo Credits: Alamy, Getty Images, iStock, Shutterstock
Production Contributors: Kenny Abdo, Jennie Forsberg, Grace Hansen
Design Contributors: Dorothy Toth, Neil Klinepier

Library of Congress Control Number: 2017960642

Publisher's Cataloging-in-Publication Data

Names: Abdo, Kenny, author.
Title: How to survive a blizzard / by Kenny Abdo.
Description: Minneapolis, Minnesota : Abdo Zoom, 2019. | Series: How to survive |
     Includes online resources and index.
Identifiers: ISBN 9781532123238 (lib.bdg.) | ISBN 9781532124211 (ebook) |
     ISBN 9781532124709 (Read-to-me ebook)
Subjects: LCSH: Survival--Juvenile literature. | Blizzards--Juvenile literature. |
     Emergencies--Planning--Juvenile literature. | Natural disasters--
     Juvenile literature.
Classification: DDC 613.69--dc23

TABLE OF CONTENTS

BLIZZARDS

A blizzard is a **snowstorm** with strong winds of at least 35 mph (56 km/h). It can last for three or more hours.

The blizzard of 1993, also known as the "Storm of the Century," brought strong winds, snow, and very cold temperatures. Some parts of the United States' east coast saw more than 40 inches (101.6 cm) of snow! Millions of homes lost power and some people lost their lives.

PREPARE

A blizzard can trap you at home for many days. It can also cause loss of electricity and heat.

It is important to be prepared. A flashlight, bottled water, and canned food will be useful to you. An alternative heating source, like a fireplace or blankets, will keep you warm.

You should always keep emergency **supplies** in your car. A first-aid kit, shovel, compass, blankets, flares, and water are some good things to have.

Winter Driving Checklist

- [ ] Flashlight
- [ ] First Aid Kit
- [ ] Snow Shovel
- [ ] Booster Cables
- [ ] Flares/Triangles
- [ ] Extra food and water
- [ ] Warm clothing/blankets
- [ ] Sand/Kitty Litter

SURVIVE

During a blizzard, you should stay indoors at all times. Pets should come inside too. And farm animals must be sheltered from the storm.

It is best not to travel by car or on foot in a blizzard. If it is necessary, you should put on several layers of clothing. Gloves, warm socks, and boots will protect your fingers and toes. Covering your mouth will help protect your lungs.

Always be aware of signs of **frostbite** and **hypothermia**. Signs of frostbite include loss of feeling in your fingers, toes, and the tip of your nose. Signs of hypothermia include shivering, memory loss, and exhaustion.

If your car is caught in a blizzard, stay in it. Do not try to walk to safety. Try to signal for help with either flares, warning triangles, or a ribbon tied outside of your car. Get back in your car and wait for rescuers.

GLOSSARY

frostbite – injury to body tissues caused by exposure to extreme cold.

hypothermia – the condition of having an abnormally low body temperature, typically one that is dangerously low.

snowstorm – a heavy snowfall with very strong wind.

supplies – things that are needed to do something.

temperature – how hot or cold it is outside. Measured in Fahrenheit and Celsius degrees.

ONLINE RESOURCES

Booklinks
NONFICTION NETWORK
FREE! ONLINE NONFICTION RESOURCES

To learn more about surviving a blizzard, please visit abdobooklinks.com. These links are routinely monitored and updated to provide the most current information available.

INDEX